THE RHS GARDEN ROSEMOOR

The Royal Horticultural Society's West Country regional centre and garden at Ro⟨ ⟩

provides a focal point for the Society's activities in the region, and a garden for visito⟨ ⟩

enjoy at all times of the year. Rosemoor Garden is designed to demonstrate the widest

range of horticultural practice and planting appropriate to the area. As such it is not only a showpiece, but has a key role as a practical demonstration garden from which visitors can draw both inspiration and instruction. Rosemoor

also provides a lesson in what may be achieved over a brief time scale, as the new garden

area (effectively three-quarters of the estate), has been developed comparatively recently,

with the first plantings having been made in 1990.

Alongside the delights of the garden, Rosemoor is also an active centre for RHS

members and gardeners whatever their interests throughout the region. Additional pro-

grammes at Rosemoor and Cannington College include

garden walks, lectures, workshops and demonstrations

of gardening and related topics such as botanical paint-

ing and country crafts. A full programme of events and

exhibitions adds greatly to the interest of any visit.

THE GUIDE

Our guide to the RHS Garden Rosemoor takes you on a tour of the garden, from the Robin Herbert Centre through to the South Arboretum. We have introduced a circular route which visits all the gardens in the Formal Garden and a similar route in Lady Anne's Garden, but of course visitors are free to choose their own route and the map key (opposite) identifies each area of Rosemoor. For ease of reference within the guide, the map key has been ordered to match the circular route described above.

The map has been colour coded to distinguish the five distinct areas of the garden around which the guide is based. Each map section is repeated at the start of each of the five areas as a quick reference, and continued in miniature on the relevant pages throughout that section.

We hope you enjoy your visit to Rosemoor and find this booklet a useful and informative guide to this important national garden.

The story of Rosemoor Garden begins for us in 1959 when Lady Anne Berry (Lady Anne Palmer) caught measles from her children and, while recuperating in Spain, met the noted plantsman Collingwood Ingram. He invited her to visit his garden on her return to England and encouraged her to return to Rosemoor with a few of his plants to start a garden of her own.

Lady Anne's garden, as this area of Rosemoor is now known, is a plantsman's garden and is of great horticultural and botanical interest. Inspired by the enthusiasm of plantsman Collingwood Ingram, the garden development continued with the planting of specimens collected by Lady Anne on her travels all over Europe, Australia, New Zealand, Papua New Guinea, Japan, the USA and temperate South America. All the new introductions have been carefully labelled and their origin documented to provide the collection with its fascinating history.

In 1923 Lady Anne's parents bought the Rosemoor estate as a family fishing lodge to be used only through March to May. Originally part of the Rolle estate (a local Devon family), it was at that time owned by a Colonel Graham and rented by a Major Rustin. Both were fishermen and in those days the Torridge was a very good salmon river.

Following the death of her father in 1931 it became home to Lady Anne and her mother. At that time the garden was

This cherry tree photographed in Lady Anne's Garden in 1988, just before the Society received the garden, is a testament to her mentor Collingwood Ingram. Now a mature specimen it can be seen near to the house

Originally built as a reservoir, the Lake is a magical area for all seasons

ROSEMOOR

The main vista from the terrace to the woodland through the Formal Garden is a breathtaking introduction to the garden

Nets provide protection against birds and animals for cabbages and sprouts in the Fruit and Vegetable Garden

as Lady Anne describes it "dull and labour-intensive, typically Victorian with a great use of annuals in beds round the house".

In 1932 the Stone Garden was built from a patch of rough land which led from the lane bank to the lawn. Designed by Lady Anne's mother, it was built by their chauffeur-handyman and woodman who collected stone from the limekiln (which is situated below the garden's nursery site) for the wall; slate slabs for the paving were found elsewhere on the estate. The lions on the grinding stone and carved in the wall are believed to be a Rolle family emblem and these were collected by Lady Anne's mother from local antique shops. Teak pillars taken from the *SS Revenge* which was dismantled earlier this century at Bideford port originally supported the temple roof (now sadly dismantled as the supports had become unsafe).

In 1947 Lady Anne returned to live permanently at Rosemoor with her husband and young son and found a house in need of modernisation and farm buildings in serious need of repair. For a number of years they ran the estate as a dairy farm with a herd of up to 50 Ayrshire cows until the herd was sold and the farm reverted to pasture land rented out to local farmers for grazing. The grass lets continued until 1988 when the 16ha (40 acre) estate was generously given to the Royal Horticultural Society.

When Lady Anne gave the Rosemoor estate to the RHS in 1988 it consisted of the 3.2ha (8 acre) garden around the house and 13ha (32 acres) of pasture land. The Society's plan for the site was to increase the garden area to its full size, while at the same time making Rosemoor the RHS Regional Centre for the West Country and the focal point for the Society's activities.

Rosemoor Garden is composed of two distinct areas: the original garden – Lady Anne's Garden – and the new garden area, effectively all of the estate apart from Lady Anne's original garden. The whole site is bisected by the B3220 road. Major construction was needed in the first year to link the two parts of the garden with an under-pass which leads visitors safely under the road into either side of the garden.

In 1989 work began on building the new visitors' centre, named the Robin Herbert Centre for the Society's President at the time Rosemoor was acquired by the RHS. This modern building, with its panoramic views across the garden, incorporates a shop, plant sales area, restaurant and lecture theatre. A new entrance road, car park and maintenance tracks were also needed and it is difficult now to imagine how these could have emerged from rough pasture land.

Major earthworks were required to transform the 3ha (7½ acre) square field into the Formal Garden area. Drainage and water supply systems had to be incorporated as well as electricity, gas,

Formerly pasture land for sheep (top) the Formal Garden has emerged as a garden of distinction. The view from a hot air balloon (right) shows clearly the formal patterns of the gardens

telephones and sewerage for the Robin Herbert Centre. At the same time the sloping field was cleared of its grazing sheep and then regraded to fall evenly, as was essential for the building of a formal garden, and the ground prepared for planting. For many months, the sea of mud bore no resemblance to its former occupation nor to its future as a national garden.

Another major undertaking was the building of the reservoir, the diversion of the stream and finally the rock gully (see pages 16-17).

THE SITE

Lying 1.6km (one mile) south of the town of Great Torrington on the west-facing slopes of the Torridge valley, Rosemoor sits at around 30m (98½ft) above sea level and is enclosed on all sides by woodland. It was to ensure the continued beauty of Rosemoor's surroundings, that the Society, through the generosity of its members and with the help of other donations, purchased most of the woodland that surrounds you from wherever you look in the garden.

The soil is a moderately acid, heavy, silty clay loam with a pH of around 5.5. Rainfall averages 1010mm (40in) per year and, although the climate is fairly mild overall, the valley bottom is a frost pocket and can suffer from temperatures of -9°C (16°F) or below in winter. Damage from late spring frosts is also possible, particularly in the new garden area.

After several seasons' growth in the Formal Garden it became apparent that the yew hedges enclosing each of the gardens were not happy in Rosemoor soil and they developed root disease.

To overcome the problem, a combination plan of both replacing the soil and replacing the hedges was chosen. The yew lining the central vista now grows in replaced soil, while elsewhere in the garden, hedges comprise alternate plants of holly (*Ilex aquifolium* 'J.C. van Tol') and box (*Buxus sempervirens*), with the box filling out any gaps which appear in the holly.

A reservoir to supply water for the garden was built in 1990 (above) and the natural stream diverted through a series of waterfalls to fall into the lake. The diversity of the waterside planting is outstanding and provides interest throughout the year, here (left) pictured in October

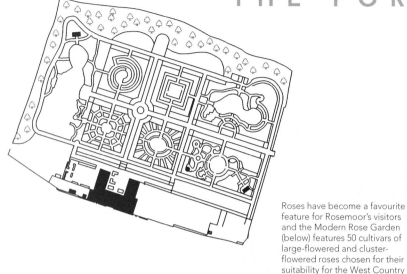

The Robin Herbert Centre stands on a west-facing terrace overlooking the Formal Garden. The terrace wall, on either side of the steps leading to the gardens, serves as shelter to many climbers and Southern Hemisphere plants while to the south of the Restaurant the Alpine Terrace is host to a display of inspiringly planted stone troughs.

FORMAL GARDEN

The Formal Garden area is the most intensively cultivated area at Rosemoor and occupies the entire 3ha (7½ acre) site. Designed on a grid system with two main axes leading east-west from the Robin Herbert Centre and north-south along the middle of the area, it has four formal gardens at its heart. To the north of these lie a semi-formal garden and a garden of rooms, with a naturalistic garden as well as model gardens to the south.

Roses have become a favourite feature for Rosemoor's visitors and the Modern Rose Garden (below) features 50 cultivars of large-flowered and cluster-flowered roses chosen for their suitability for the West Country

Rosa 'Mary Rose'

ROSE GARDENS

Immediately below the terrace the first two formal squares, dedicated to roses, were planted in spring 1990. The clean air and rather soft and damp growing conditions which prevail in the West Country make diseases such as mildew, black spot and rust a particular problem for rose growers in this part of the country. Here, cultivars have been carefully chosen for resistance to disease and they provide inspiration to all West Country gardeners.

The Modern Roses on the left (south-west) feature over 50 cultivars. Large-flowered (hybrid tea) and cluster-flowered (floribunda) roses predominate with a mixture of climbers to clothe the obelisk-shaped pillars. As well as disease resistance, the cultivars have also been chosen for their scent and to represent a range of sizes and colours.

ROSES OF INTEREST

Modern Roses
Amber Queen
City of London
Escapade
Iceberg

Savoy Hotel
Trumpeter

Shrub Roses
Bonica

Graham Thomas
Heritage
Jacqueline du Pré
Mary Rose
'De Rescht'

A catenary is a major feature of the Shrub Roses, to the right (north-east) of the Modern Rose Garden, and stronger-growing cultivars are trained along the rope which joins the pillars. The groups of roses in this garden represent the story of shrub roses from its beginnings to the present day, with modern hybrids such as the English roses demonstrating the up-to-the-minute developments in breeding. In all, 130 cultivars can be found among the nearly 500 roses. Pruning in both these gardens is carried out by hand with secateurs during the winter months, with the modern roses being left until the end. This takes a team of gardeners several weeks.

POTAGER, HERB AND COTTAGE GARDENS

The traditionally built thatched summerhouse in the Cottage Garden highlighted by spring bulbs

Three distinct gardens are contained in the area to the north of the Shrub Roses. A dry stone wall built in a West Country style bisects the area, with the Herb Garden and Potager to the south and Cottage Garden to the north. Each area has strong elements of landscaping and planting in common.

HERB GARDEN

The plantings in the Herb Garden cover the entire range of medicinal, culinary and other herbs while the garden has been designed to incorporate many features for the disabled. Despite the sloping site the use of steps has been avoided and the bricks used in the paths provide a good all-weather surface. Parking bays for wheelchairs have been provided and the raised beds allow many plants to be seen and appreciated more closely.

POTAGER

With a name appropriated from the French term *Jardin Potager*, the Potager is effectively an ornamental kitchen garden. Four beds are arranged in a circle, enclosed with a number of tall wrought-iron arches, each supporting a cultivar of grape vine. A central arch supports two species of

Wisteria. In the beds, vegetables have been arranged in groups to demonstrate contrasting foliage, form and colour.

COTTAGE GARDEN

The principal feature of the Cottage Garden is an authentically constructed thatched summer-house, built of local oak without the use of screws or nails, and with walls of wattle and daub. Spring bulbs bring colour and interest to the garden from February and are superseded by an exuberant mixture of colourful and scented plants. Occasional vegetables and fruit can also be found among the more decorative plantings and a small collection of local apple cultivars provides both blossom and fruit interest in the orchard in the north-west corner of the garden.

Left: feverfew and *Lavandula angustifolia* 'Munstead' edge one of the Herb Garden's pathways

Below: the distinctive wrought-iron arches in the Potager supports *Wisteria floribunda* 'Multijuga' and *W. floribunda* 'Royal Purple'. Grape vines clothe the outer circle of arches

The elements of hard land-scaping and design which connect these three gardens are clearly visible in this view through the Potager, Herb and Cottage Gardens. The Herb Garden is in the fore-ground, Potager in the centre and Cottage at the rear

9

PLANTSMAN'S GARDEN PLANTS OF INTEREST

Desfontainia spinosa
Dicentra
Eucryphia
Francoa sonchifolia
Magnolia x veitchii
Mahonia x media 'Lionel Fortescue'

Right: the beauty of the shapes and colours of grasses is emphasized alongside the flowing path at the rear of the Foliage and Plantsman's Garden

Below: slate sculptures bring a contrasting formality to the naturalistic Foliage and Plantsman's Garden with their upright nobility echoed by *Kniphofia* 'Green Jade' in the foreground

Opposite: the foliage garden at its best in autumn. Soft light filters through the flowers of pampas grass and enhances the glowing pink *Sedum*

The flowing paths and lines reflect the emphasis on natural form in the Foliage Garden, where the contrasting shapes and colours of plant and leaf provide interest over a prolonged season. Grasses and grass-like plants are strongly represented illustrating a range of leaf colours from greens and blues to red, brown, gold and many types of variegation. In late summer/early autumn the garden is further enhanced by the beauty of the grass flowers such as *Miscanthus* and pampas grasses (*Cortaderia* species). Clipped and trained plants provide strong contrasts to the natural flowing contours. Pleached hornbeam, box pillars and an area of espaliered *Sorbus thibetica* 'John Mitchell' all add distinctive textural notes. A series of standing slates in the south-east corner of the garden are intended to provide a formal sculptural element contrasting with the flowing lines of the local stone paths and raised beds.

A dry stone planting bed for alpines and dwarf shrubs divides the Foliage and Plantsman's Gardens. The Plantman's Garden has been designed to enable the widest range of interesting and unusual plants to be accommodated, many of West Country origin, in conditions ranging from woodland to open and sunny.

10

Two colour themed gardens lie side by side in the Formal Garden area providing a contrast in both colour and internal design. The tall yew hedges enclose both gardens, hiding their secrets from the other and the move from the Square to the Spiral calms senses battered by the riot of colour in the Square Garden. Both gardens illustrate exciting herbaceous perennial and shrub planting combinations of which many elements could be copied for use in domestic gardens.

Coreopsis, hemerocallis and dahlias bring vibrant colour to the Square Garden

SQUARE GARDEN

Hot colours predominate in the Square Garden, an area of rigidly divided beds, with a vibrant mixture of red, orange, yellow and purple. These colours contrast well with the bright foliage of the shrubs and trees which have been planted to provide structural interest. The central area, a small, intimate enclosure, has the hottest colours.

PLANTS OF INTEREST

In the Square Garden
Buddleja davidii 'Dartmoor'
Canna 'Roi Humbert'
Dahlia 'Bishop of Llandaff'
Lobelia 'Bees' Flame'
Robinia pseudoacacia 'Frisia'
Rudbeckia 'Goldsturm'

In the Spiral Garden
Artemisia
Aster ericoides cultivars
Lupinus 'Polar Princess'
Miscanthus sinensis 'Variegatus'
Phlomis fruticosa
Ptelea trifoliata 'Aurea'

SPIRAL GARDEN

From the hot squares of the Square Garden a complete contrast in design and colour is found in the Spiral Garden. The path winds in towards its centre ending in a paved area containing two semi-circular seats. Shrubs provide the backbone to the borders whose colours flow around the garden from pale yellow and green through pale blue to mauve and violet, then pink, peach and apricot to yellow again. By the time the seats in the centre are reached the colours gradually fade to the restful tones of white and grey.

Above: a panoramic view of the Square Garden best illustrates the skilled colour combinations of red, yellow, orange and purple. The dark green background of hedge and woodland emphasizes the power of these hot colours

The cool tones of the Spiral Garden fade to white and grey at its centre providing a tranquil surrounding to the paved seating area. Here the daisy-like *Leucanthemum* x *superbum* 'Phyllis Smith' is accompanied by *Lychnis* and *Malva moschata* f. *alba*

Right: the coloured stems of stooled *Cornus* and *Salix* provide the backbone of colour in the Winter Garden

Below: lining both sides of the north-south axis of the Formal Garden is the Long Border. In this, the first area of the border, the colour scheme is of pale mauves, pinks and yellows.

WINTER GARDEN

In the south-west corner of the field the Winter Garden demonstrates the range of plants available whose beauty of leaf, form, fruit, bark, stem and flower, provides particular interest during the winter months. Preparation for the garden in 1996 was extensive, and required stripping the turf from what remained of the square field, followed by level-

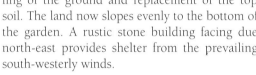

ling of the ground and replacement of the top soil. The land now slopes evenly to the bottom of the garden. A rustic stone building facing due north-east provides shelter from the prevailing south-westerly winds.

MODEL GARDENS

The first of the model gardens, A West Country

Town Garden designed by Lisa Camps, was completed in spring 1998. This garden features paths and terraces of dark grey slate and sea-washed pebbles in contrasting patterns designed to offset the blue, grey and purple foliage of much of the structural planting. Like much of the planting at Rosemoor the garden has a strong representation of structural shrubs and grasses chosen to provide as long a season of display as possible. Two more model gardens are planned for this area and all will share a central lawn. See p24 for more information on future development.

LONG BORDER

Along the north-south axis of the Formal Garden area, between the upper and lower formal squares, runs a double herbaceous border. Divided into sections within low hedged 'walls', the border has been designed to provide colour from late spring until autumn. The individual borders may also be seen as a part of the greater border from a distance and have a strong backbone of shrub planting, with long drifts of herbaceous plants to the rear, becoming more intimate in scale towards the front. The colour scheme of the first section uses flowers of mainly pink, mauve-blue, white and soft yellow, with silver, blue and purple foliage. As the border leads northwards the colour mix gradually changes, lessening in intensity and finally fading to cream and white as this majestic border leads out into the Stream Garden Field.

FRUIT GARDEN FIELD

Cross over the stream and lake and take time to visit the Fruit Garden Field.

FRUIT AND VEGETABLE GARDEN

Opened in spring 1994 it demonstrates techniques of growing and training a variety of fruit and vegetables. A 2.4m (8ft) high wall dressed with local stone provides sheltered conditions for many trained fruit trees and to the south and west a split chestnut paling fence provides a permeable boundary allowing frost to drain away and providing support for fruit trees. A rustic thatched arbour, echoing the style of that in the Cottage Garden, sits in the centre of the north wall. Within the garden a three-year rotation for vegetables is employed and a fruit cage accommodates a domestic scale planting.

FRUIT GARDEN FIELD

To the north of the Fruit and Vegetable Garden stands a small orchard specialising in top fruit cultivars for local conditions. Between this and the Lake and Stream lies the Fruit Garden Field which has been planted with ornamental fruiting trees, many with edible fruits, such as almonds.

To educate and inspire, the fruit and vegetable garden illustrates techniques for growing on a domestic scale using cultivars suitable for local conditions

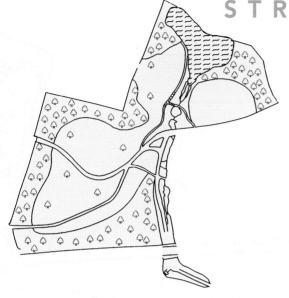

A natural stream runs through Rosemoor from Lady Anne's Garden to the Lake on the western border of the estate. It was diverted in 1990 to run through a series of shallow pools and over a number of mini-waterfalls and cascades to run under a bridge and observation platform. Water from the pools feeds several large areas of marginal and bog planting which stretch along the entire length of the stream. From the bridge two more substantial ponds and a bog garden complete the stream's gentle fall into the lake. A pipe from the lake to the top of the stream recirculates water during the summer months when the stream tends to run dry.

NATIONAL COLLECTION OF CORNUS

Rosemoor is the holder of the National Collection of *Cornus*. Many *Cornus* species may be found in Lady Anne's Garden but examples of coloured-stemmed dogwoods are visible around the lake
Cornus alba 'Kesselringii' (purple stems)
Cornus alba 'Sibirica' (red stems)
Cornus sanguinea 'Midwinter Fire' (orange stems)
Cornus stolonifera 'Flaviramea' (green stems)

Above: the pink feathery plumes of *Astilbe* in the foreground are part of the very diverse marginal planting of the bog garden in summer

Right: in winter, part of the National Collection of coloured-stemmed *Cornus* is clearly visible on the Lake perimeters

Arisaema
birches
hellebores
Indocalamus tessellatus
maples
Phyllostachys vivax
'Aureocaulis'
Phyllostachys nigra
Phyllostachys bambusoides
'Castilloni'
Tricyrtis
woodrushes

At the entrance to Lady
Anne's Garden from the
underpass , the rock gully
planting has been continued
around a small waterfall with
ferns, bamboos and
woodland perennials

BOG AND LAKE

In 1990 a dam was built at the end of the narrow valley lying on the western boundary of the garden to provide a reservoir for the garden. Holding 400,000 gallons of water, the reservoir (lake) has subsequently been planted with a wide range of marginal and aquatic plants, including water lilies. Some of the National Collection of coloured-stemmed dogwoods (*Cornus alba, C. stolonifera* and *C. sanguinea*) can be seen around the edges of the lake where they provide added interest in winter.

ROCK GULLY

Heading in an upstream direction from the lake is the underpass track leading to Lady Anne's Garden. The initial building work to provide a safe access to both areas of the garden took place in 1989 but in autumn 1995 the area was land-scaped with boulders to achieve the effect of walking through a deep rocky gully. More than 500 tonnes of local stone, some weighing 6 tonnes, have transformed the grass bank into this spectacular ravine. In spring 1996 the small planting pockets between the stones were filled with a rich, moisture-retentive woodland soil mix before the many ferns, bamboos and woodland perennials were planted. Careful soil preparation is one of the main features of Rosemoor's garden management and continues to provide an excellent starting point for new plants.

On the Lady Anne's Garden side of the underpass the use of boulder work is continued around a waterfall to form a small grotto. The tree cover above and the continuation of the rock gully style of planting has already made this a welcome shady retreat and a tranquil point of entry into the older part of the garden.

Pictured in July 1997 only
18 months after planting, the
stream and Rock Gully have
already become a well
established and exciting area
of the garden

A wide lawn leads down to Rosemoor House whose white walls are emphasized by the greens of the lawn, trees and shrubs

On entering this area of the garden it is hard to believe that much of the planting is less than 40 years old. Inspired by a meeting with Collingwood 'Cherry' Ingram, Lady Anne's real interest in gardening began in 1959. Many of the cherry trees which provide fresh spring colour, as well as many other woody plants, have been raised from cuttings and layers which were a gift from Collingwood Ingram's own garden. Also strongly featured in Lady Anne's Garden is part of Rosemoor's National Collections of *Ilex* and *Cornus*.

The track from the Underpass joins the Main Drive which effectively bisects this area of the garden. To the left

G A R D E N

Left: the bank between the Croquet Lawn and the Tennis Court in the 1930s. The old oak in the background is still thriving today

Below: the front of the house provides a sheltered microclimate for the tender climbers which accompany *Clematis, Wisteria* and *Rosa banksiae* Lutea

(west) is the Main Lawn while to the east and south of the house an area of divided gardens has gradually been developed by Lady Anne from the former croquet lawn, tennis court and kitchen garden and other areas of the garden.

THE MAIN LAWN

Flanked on either side by planting, the Main Lawn runs the length of the vista to Rosemoor House. Moving along the lawn the beds to the right are each planted to follow a colour theme, the first with yellow, orange and bronze flowers and purple foliage, and the second white and silver. The plantings to the left contain a mix of rhododendrons, camellias and magnolias. This mix continues along Lock's Trail, a woodland walk from the main lawn to the old car park west of the house, emerging through a planting of Knap Hill hybrid azaleas. This area is at its most colourful in early summer.

ROSEMOOR HOUSE

The House, built around the 1780s, was extended by Lady Anne's father to accommodate more staff and later modernized internally by Lady Anne and her husband after the Second World War. During the war it was used by the Red Cross as a temporary refuge from the bombing for people from London's Docklands and East End. Today, the west wing is used for staff offices with the remainder of the building taken up by staff accommodation.

The south-westerly facing aspect of the front of the house provides perfect, sheltered conditions for many tender plants, such as *Acacia dealbata*, grevilleas and *Olearia insignis*.

Right: the naturally acid soil in the Woodland Garden is ideal for ericaceous plants such as rhododendrons and azaleas, which bring this area of the garden to life in late spring

A framework of hardy plants in the Kitchen Garden is joined in summer by banana palms and shrubby salvias for true sub-tropical splendour

In the old Kitchen Garden to the side of the House sub-tropical planting can be found. Hardy plants, such as *Cordyline, Phormium* and hardy palms (*Trachycarpus*) with hedychiums (ginger lilies), create a sub-tropical framework which is then enhanced with tender plants, such as the banana palm (*Musa basjoo*) and variegated *Arundo donax,* during the summer months. The plants are carefully lifted and potted in October before the first frosts and housed in the Nursery at a temperature of not less than 5°C (41°F), being replanted towards the end of May after the last frost.

CHERRY GARDEN

This area takes its name from the mature Japanese cherries growing here. In recent years it has been extensively redeveloped as a woodland garden with a wide range of choice perennials not represented in the more woody plantings of the Woodland Garden proper.

WOODLAND GARDEN

Lying east of the Old Kitchen Garden, the Woodland Garden has been created on a steep west-facing slope. A woodland walk high on the slope offers wonderful views over Lady Anne's Garden and of the surrounding hills beyond. This area contains some of the original Collingwood Ingram cherry introductions, as well as many ericaceous plants and is at its most colourful in

Left: the stone lion remains in place today in the Stone Garden. This is one of the oldest parts of the garden and has changed little in the last 60 years

Below: the recently completed Stone Garden photographed around 1932-33.

spring. This feature is being extended, incorporating the site of Lady Anne's original nursery.

STONE GARDEN

This is one of the oldest parts of the garden with the temple and pathways designed by Lady Anne's mother in 1932. Although the garden has changed much in its development during Lady Anne's time and with the Society, all the hard landscaping in the Stone Garden is still in place, including the lion on the grinding stone, but the

temple roof was recently dismantled as the original teak supports were found to be unsafe. Early colour photographs show a subtantial bush of *Paeonia suffruticosa* var. *rockii* at the foot of the temple. This magnificent shrub still flowers today.

CROQUET LAWN

Originally, as one may expect, this area was the family's croquet lawn until Lady Anne expanded the garden's boundaries and began to develop the surrounding beds. The microclimate in this area provides ideal conditions for many unusual evergreens and southern hemisphere plants, including South American, Tasmanian, Chilean and New Zealand subjects. In 1996 the main bank of the Croquet Lawn area, just below and in the shelter of the Woodland Garden was extended and refurbished. The old oak tree which stands on the bank between the Croquet Lawn and Tennis Court features in old photographs of the garden in the 1930s. In those days it was already a mature specimen.

TENNIS COURT

The initial plantings in the Tennis Court were made in 1979 and the whole area was revised and replanted in 1994, with further improvements made annually. A spectacular *Eucalyptus glaucescens* in the south-east corner is surrounded by many Australasian plants. Self-sown seedlings of this eucalypt can be seen throughout the centre of the Tennis Court. This sheltered site is home to a selection of fast growing plants from Mediterranean climates such as California, New Zealand, Australia, South Africa and the Mediterranean itself. Raised beds provide better drained conditions, essential in this otherwise wet locality, and soil preparation in this area has included the incorporation of large quantities of grit to improve the drainage. In this poor soil the growth of plants is hard, which assists them in surviving the occasional cold spell.

MEDITERRANEAN AND AUSTRALASIAN PLANTS

Corokia x *virgata*
Cordateria richardii
Cytisus x *beanii*
Euphorbia myrsinites
Grevillea juniperina f. *sulphurea*
Hebe 'Pewter Dome'
Hoheria sexstylosa
Olearia nummulariifolia
Ozothamnus rosmarinifolius 'Silver Jubilee'
Phlomis anatolica 'Lloyd's Variety'
Phormium cookianum subsp. *hookeri* 'Tricolor'
Pinus pinea
Pittosporum tenuifolium 'Abbotsbury Gold'
Podocarpus totara 'Pendulus'
Stipa gigantea
Yucca whipplei

Above: Australasian and Mediterranean plants predominate in the Old Tennis Court where raised beds and quantities of grit have improved drainage and helped these warm temperate plants to survive

Left: the shape of things to come – compare this self-sown seedling with the mature tree of *Eucalyptus glaucescens* on a visit to the Tennis Court area

ARBORETA

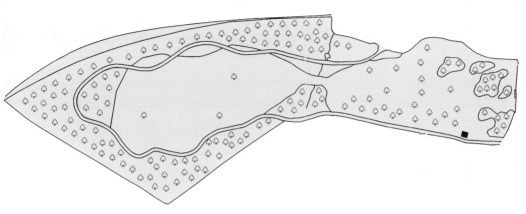

ARBORETUM

The plantings in this area include many rare trees and shrubs planted by Lady Anne, and extend to the valley of the spring which once marked the previous southern boundary of the garden. Much of the planting began in 1975, with many grown from wild-collected seed. Trees have been planted deliberately close together with a view to thinning out as they grow.

SOUTH ARBORETUM

The triangular field beyond the Arboretum has the best natural drainage and finest soil of the entire Rosemoor estate. It is being developed as an informal area with plantings following broad geographical themes: North American and Asiatic species predominating along the eastern and southern edges, a large ericaceous garden in the south-west corner of the field and European and near-Eastern species by the Upper Bog Garden. Initially the area has been planted with a nursery planting of fast-growing trees. These will provide shelter for the permanent framework of trees and shrubs to be incorporated over the next 10 years.

Acer rubrum 'October Glory' lives up to its name in the Arboretum

TREES OF INTEREST IN THE ARBORETUM

birches
Carya (hickory)
Juglans nigra (walnut)
maples
Nothofagus (southern beech)
Pterocarya (wingnut)
Quercus
Sorbus
Zelkova

FUTURE DEVELOPMENTS

In the area alongside the Modern Roses, a new development of model gardens is planned. The gardens will share a central lawn, and although designed separately and by different designers it is intended that they are viewed as a whole. Designed by members of the Society of Garden Designers, styles will range from a garden for shade, lying alongside the wooded southern edge of the field, a contemporary terrace immediately west of the Robin Herbert Centre and the West Country Town Garden opened in spring 1998. The two remaining gardens will be built in 1999 and 2000.

Following an appeal to local members the Society now owns some 32.5ha (80 acres) of mixed woodland and forestry plantations surrounding the garden. It is intended that these will, over time, be returned to mixed natural woodland and that visitors to the Garden will have access to them. Over the next five years woodland walks above Lady Anne's Garden and west of the Formal Garden are planned.

AMENITIES

EVENTS

Alongside the development of a national garden, Rosemoor is the RHS Regional Centre for the West Country. Centred upon Rosemoor and Cannington College in Bridgwater, Somerset, RHS members may attend garden walks, demonstrations, workshops and lectures as well as seek advice on garden problems. Activities for children have also proved very popular here with the early instigation of Rosemoor Junior and Senior Explorers' trails encouraging young children to take an interest in plants, how they grow and their different functions. Packs for teachers are also available and organized school visits are offered.

FACILITIES

Disabled people are well catered for. Limited numbers of wheelchairs are available free of charge at the entrance and can be booked in advance, early on the day of visit, if required. Admission is free for helpers of wheelchair-bound and blind visitors. Most of the garden is accessible to wheelchair users.

The Robin Herbert Centre incorporates a lecture theatre, self-service licensed restaurant, plant centre and gift shop. The Plant Centre sells an excellent selection of top quality plants and the shop stocks a wide range of both the beautiful and useful, from books to kitchenware.

The self-service restaurant serves a wide range of hot and cold food and is open from 2 January to 24 December.